BRUCH'S "KOL NIDREI"
AND
BLOCH'S "SCHELOMO"

for Cello and Orchestra
in Full Score

Max Bruch

Ernest Bloch

Dover Publications, Inc.
New York

Bibliographical Note

This Dover edition, first published in 1996, is a new compilation of two scores originally published separately in authoritative editions, n.d.: *Max Bruch, Op. 47 / Kol Nidrei / Adagio for Violoncello* [sic], and *Ernest Bloch / "Schelomo" / Rhapsodie hébraïque pour Violoncelle solo et Grand Orchestre.*

The Dover edition adds lists of contents and instrumentation, an editorial note and an English translation of the footnote on p. 62.

International Standard Book Number: 0-486-29039-5

Manufactured in the United States of America
Dover Publications, Inc., 31 East 2nd Street, Mineola, N.Y. 11501

Contents

Note

Kol Nidre ("all vows") is the Aramaic prayer sung in synagogues on the eve of Yom Kippur, the Day of Atonement, Judaism's most solemn holy day. The name—derived from the initial words of an ancient text expressing repentance for unfulfilled promises made to God—also designates the melody to which the prayer is traditionally chanted.

In his "Kol Nidrei" (a variant spelling), Protestant composer Max Bruch uses a version of a melody of unknown origin sung in the Ashkenazi (German) rite.

Schelomo, the Hebrew name for Solomon, is Ernest Bloch's musical portrait of the legendary poet, sage and king—the son and successor of David—traditionally regarded as the most powerful ruler of Israel. The only written record of his bold and energetic forty-year reign, thought to be in the mid-10th century B.C., is in the Bible, especially 1 Kings and 2 Chronicles.

"Kol Nidrei"
INSTRUMENTATION

2 Flutes [Flöten]
2 Oboes [Hoboen]
2 Clarinets in A [Clarinetten]
2 Bassoons [Fagotte]

4 Horns in D [Hörner]
2 Trumpets in D [Trompeten]
3 Trombones [Posaunen]

Timpani [Pauken]

Cello Solo [Violoncell-Solo]

Violins I, II [Violine]
Violas [Bratsche]
Cellos [Violoncell]
Basses [Bass]

Harp [Harfe]

"Schelomo"
INSTRUMENTATION

3 Flutes [Flauto, Fl.]
    Fl. III doubles Piccolo [Ottavino]
2 Oboes [Oboe, Ob.]
English Horn [Corno inglese, Cor. ingl.]
2 Clarinets in B♭ [Clarinetto, Cl. (Si♭)]
Bass Clarinet [Clarinetto basso, Cl. bss.]
2 Bassoons [Fagotto, Fag.]
Contrabassoon [Contrafagotto, C.-fag.]

4 Horns in F [Corni, Cor. (Fa)]
3 Trumpets in C [Tromba, Tba/e. (Do)]
3 Trombones [Trombone, Tbne., Tbe.]
Tuba [Tuba]

Timpani [Timpani, Timp.]

Percussion:
    Tambourine [Tambour de basque]
    Snare Drum [Tamburo]
    Bass Drum [Gr(an) cassa, Gr. c.]
    Cymbals [Piatti]
    Tam-tam [Tam-tam]

Celesta [Celesta, Cel.]
2 Harps [Arpa]

Cello Solo [Violoncello (Vcl.) solo]

Violin I [Violino, Vln.] (*at least 12 players*)
Violin II [Violino, Vln.] (*at least 10*)
Violas [Viole, Vle.] (*at least 8*)
Cellos [Violoncelli, Vcelli, Vcl.] (*at least 6*)
Basses [Contrabassi, C.-bss., Cbss.) (*at least 4*)

"KOL NIDREI"

"SCHELOMO"

"Schelomo"

* Note pour le chef d'orchestre: battre alla breve (aussi le $\frac{7}{4}$)
* Nota pel Direttore d'orchestra: Battere alla breve (anche la $\frac{7}{4}$)

*) Note for the conductor: [At the Più animato, just after ⑰] beat each bar in two (including the 7/4).